the byron bay

cookbook

victoria mcewen

photography and styling **david young**

text **fay knight**

Byron Bay Publishing

Publishers: Raemon and Victoria McEwen, David Young

Byron Bay Publishing

Top of McGettigans Lane, Byron Bay, NSW 2481 AUSTRALIA

First published 2000

First Edition

Photographs copyright © **David Young 2000**

Whale photograph copyright © David Paton 2000

National Library of Australia cataloguing-in-publication data:

McEwen, Victoria

The Byron Bay Cookbook

Includes index

ISBN 0-646-39983-7

1. Cookery - New South Wales - Byron Bay.

2. Cookery, Australian. I. Young, David. II. Knight, Fay. III. Title

641.5099443

Design: Rebecca Kinsey, **Utopia Creative,** Byron Bay

Printed in Australia by **Fergies Image to Press,** Brisbane

contents

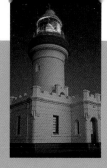

acknowledgements

This book has been a dream of mine for a long time, and as with any project of this magnitude, it wouldn't have been the publication that it is without the help of many key people.

I wish to especially thank my husband Raemon, without whose business expertise, financial backing and total support, it would not have been possible. Also David Young, for his stunning photography, and for sharing my vision, and co-producing and coordinating the entire project with me.

Victoria McEwen

David, Raemon and myself would like to thank the following:

Fay Knight, for her input and creativity in writing the text.

The team at Utopia Creative, for their brilliant design.

Madonna Duffy and David Oliver, publishers of *Noosa: the Cookbook*, for their assistance and encouragement with this project.

The chefs and restauranteurs who so willingly shared their recipes and gave up their time, to allow us to get the food shots just right!

Everyone who kindly gave us permission to use their quotes in this book:

Byron Bay: Winter, used by permission of the author, from 'New and Selected Poems' (Duffy & Snellgrove, 1998).

Quote, from the new novel by Victoria Thompson, author of 'Losing Alexandria', a memoir.

Quote, from 'Sartori', by Linda Jaivin ('Best Australian Short Stories' 1999, edited by Peter Craven; Bookman Press, 1999).

Quote, from 'Bay watch', by Craig McGregor, Good Weekend, April 3,1999.

Also with thanks to the following people and businesses for their contribution:

Shop 117, Lismore; Get Stuffed Gourmet, Bangalow and The Cape Gallery, Byron Bay for props.

Brunswick Fish Co-op, Colin Heaney Art Glass, Cougar Café, Robin King and Mick Williams.

Finally, thank you to the people of Byron Bay, who make it the unique and wonderful place that it is.

introduction

Byron Bay, located on the far north coast of New South Wales, is mainland Australia's most easterly point. A rural coastal town, whose shire includes magnificent sandy beaches, lush rolling hinterland and pristine rainforest. Visitors from all over the world have been attracted to this beautiful location for its natural environment and creative energy.

The Byron Bay Cookbook is a celebration of Byron's innovative cuisine, unique culture, natural beauty and its emergence as a cosmopolitan centre. We have featured a wide selection of imaginative dishes from some of Byron's best restaurants and chefs. We are proud to be able to say that this book has been produced locally and printed in Australia.

We are lucky here, not only do we live in the country, but also we can zip to downtown Byron Bay and indulge in a decent cappuccino or choose from a wide variety of cuisines. It's definitely the best of both worlds. Whether you're a resident, a visitor or a passionate foodie, we hope you find inspiration in *The Byron Bay Cookbook*.

Victoria McEwen
David Young

coastal

Yet until just over a hundred and thirty years ago, Byron Bay was still the sub-tropical paradise of the original inhabitants, the Arakwal people, part of the Bundjalung people who populated the northern New South Wales and south-east Queensland region. Food from the land and the sea was so abundant that the coastal tribes had time to develop a rich, cultural life. Clean air, clean food and a creative community are still important to all who live in this beautiful area.

No one knows how many other exotic foreign ships may have been sighted over the millennia before the strange, billowing sails of the Endeavour rounded the headland in 1770, but James Cook named the prominent landmark Cape Byron (not for the poet, but for the poet's grandfather, a vice-admiral). People from all over the world are still drawn to experience Byron Bay, surfers dreaming of the perfect wave, backpackers dreaming of a myriad of futures before settling down in Stockholm or Manchester, stressed-out urban refugees hoping to find a lifestyle rich in meaning beyond dollars.

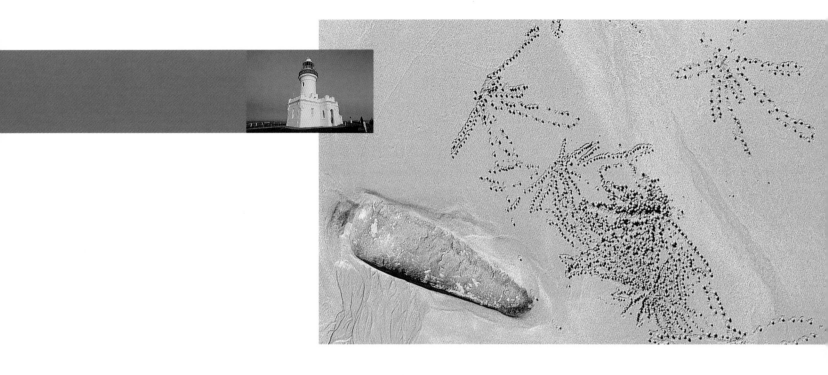

" Byron Bay to me is a very special place, it's my identity, and it's where I come from and where I will always return even when my life has ceased. My existence was created from this place and it will always be the place where I can connect with who I am, and speak to my ancestors, my creators, for guidance and reassurance.

There are many special places where I go to unwind from this ever-changing society. I rejuvenate my health and well-being by seeking my traditional tucker from the land and the sea.

Arakwal is my country – my past and my future. "

Yvonne Stewart
Arakwal representative

ingredients:

1 cup milk

3/4 cup plain flour

1 egg

20 gm butter

125 gm softened cream cheese

1 tablespoon horseradish

2 tablespoons herbs (dill, chives, parsley), finely chopped

salt and pepper

400 gm sliced smoked trout

50 gm cream cheese, extra

40 gm salmon caviar

smoked trout and crêpe roulade

Place the milk, flour and egg into a blender and process into a smooth

crêpe batter. Heat a 25 cm frypan and grease with a small amount of butter,

to prevent the crêpes from sticking. Pour some of the crêpe batter into the frypan,

coating the base evenly. Cook the crêpe until the underside is golden brown, then

turn over. When cooked, remove from the pan and keep warm. Repeat the

process with the remaining batter.

Mix together the cream cheese, horseradish, herbs, salt and pepper. Spread the

cream cheese mixture over each crêpe, and lay 2-3 slices of smoked trout over

each crêpe. Roll the crêpes tightly, wrap in foil and heat through in a warm oven.

To serve, slice the rolled crêpes into 3 cm roulades, place in the centre of a plate

and garnish with extra cream cheese and salmon caviar.

[serves: 4]

recipe : victoria mcewen : victoria's at wategos

"It's the 'all-you-can-eat' of surfing destinations," said an awed American surfer. With beaches running from Brunswick in the north, through to Belongil, Main Beach, Clarks, The Pass, Wategos and around the Cape to Tallow Beach (named for the product washed up from a shipwreck in 1864), Suffolk Park and Broken Head, somewhere there is bound to be a wave. Maybe even the perfect wave...

If you're not actually taking the waters yourself, Cape Byron, with its sturdy, century-old lighthouse, is a wonderful place to see others enjoying the ocean. Surfers, yachts, boats and pods of dolphins who surf the waves too. Whales, if you're lucky. Whaling ceased in Byron Bay in 1962, and now the annual whale migrations inspire tourist migrations.

steamed marinated fish with native finger limes

In a bowl, combine the soy sauce, sesame oil, water and the fish sauce.

Marinate the fish fillets for 10 minutes.

Mix the butter and flour with the fish stock and place into a saucepan.

Bring to the boil with the mirin, lime juice, sweet chilli sauce, chilli, ginger,

fish sauce and lemon myrtle. Gently simmer for approximately 10 minutes.

Steam the fish in a bamboo steamer, over hot water, until the fish is

cooked and tender.

Sear the watercress quickly in a hot pan with a small amount of oil.

Serve the fish on top of the watercress, spoon the sauce over the fish

and serve with the peeled finger limes.

[serves: 6]

recipe : steve snow : fins restaurant

ingredients:

6 jewfish fillets

1 bunch watercress

1 tablespoon oil

12 finger limes

marinade:

100 ml sweet soy sauce

1 teaspoon sesame oil

100 ml water

25 ml fish sauce

sauce:

50 gm butter

2 tablespoons flour

4 cups fish stock

1 cup mirin

1 cup lime juice

1/2 tablespoon sweet chilli sauce

1/2 tablespoon chilli, finely chopped

1 tablespoon ginger, julienned

1 tablespoon fish sauce

6 lemon myrtle leaves, cut finely

Byron Bay : Winter

Robert Gray

Barely contained by the eyesight,
the beach makes one great arc –
blue ranges, overlapped behind it;
each of them a tide-mark.

About me, swamp oaks' foliage
streams: hatching by Cézanne.
Off in the heath, a guard's carriage
follows the vats of a train.

A creek spoils the hem of the sea;
spread on the beach in flutes:
it has the redness of black tea,
from the swamp's sodden roots.

Behind, cloudy afternoon swells,
the colour of claret stain.
The sunlit town is strewn like shells.
Its lighthouse, a tiny pawn.

I'm walking on the beach alone;
the sea's grey feathers flurry,
showing emerald. Sandpipers blown
seem mice, in their scurry.

And the sun on my shoulders brings,
because it's perfect warmth,
the feeling that I wear great wings
while stepping along the earth.

snapper cakes

Cut the snapper fillets into 1 cm pieces. Combine the garlic, ginger, lemon grass, kaffir lime leaves and carrot in a food processor. Blend until all ingredients are finely chopped (about 3 mm in size), and place into a bowl. Mix in the snapper, beans, coriander and basil, and then the combined sugar, sweet chilli and fish sauce. When well mixed add the breadcrumbs to bind the mixture together, then roll into 4 cm balls.

Heat the peanut oil in a pan over high heat, then toss the snapper cakes in the flour and fry until golden brown. Serve with spicy dipping sauce.

[serves: 6]

ingredients:

300 gm snapper fillets

2 cloves garlic

5 cm piece ginger, peeled

1 stick lemon grass, finely chopped

2 kaffir lime leaves, finely cut

1 carrot, finely diced

12 green beans, finely cut

1/2 bunch coriander, roughly chopped

1/2 bunch basil, roughly chopped

50 gm castor sugar

1/4 cup sweet chilli sauce

1/2 teaspoon fish sauce

1/2 cup breadcrumbs

1/2 cup plain flour

1 cup peanut oil

recipe : steve snow : fins restaurant

“ I derive enormous pleasure from a swim across from The Pass to the clubhouse on Main Beach, it's one of the great swims in the world. I will always return to Byron. There's no other country town like it anywhere. ”

Rob Hirst

musician
Midnight Oil

“ Byron Bay is better than sex! ”

Ruth Ostrow
former sex writer, now spiritual affairs writer for The Australian

ingredients:

35 gm butter

3 tablespoons peanut oil

3 birds' eye chillies, finely chopped

1 lemon grass stalk, crushed and finely chopped

1 red spanish onion, finely diced

4 cloves garlic, finely chopped

1/2 bunch parsley, roughly chopped

1 teaspoon cracked black pepper

2 tablespoons fish sauce

100 ml verjuice

300 gm spanner crabmeat

800 gm linguini pasta, cooked

1/4 bunch coriander leaves

roasted tomatoes:

4 roma tomatoes, quartered lengthwise

2 tablespoons olive oil

2 tablespoons balsamic vinegar

castor sugar

sea salt

pepper

chilli spanner crab linguine

Place the cut roma tomatoes on a tray, and drizzle with the combined olive oil and balsamic vinegar. Sprinkle lightly with sugar, salt and pepper, and then roast in a 200°C oven for 1 hour.

To prepare the stock, heat the peanut oil in a large pan and cook the chilli, lemon grass, ginger, star anise, coriander roots, onion, carrot, and kaffir lime leaves, for 2 minutes. Add the water and bring to the boil, reduce the heat and simmer for 20 minutes, then strain.

Heat the butter and peanut oil in a large frypan. Add the chilli, lemon grass, onion, garlic, half the parsley and the pepper. Fry for 2 minutes on medium to high heat, until cooked. Deglaze the pan with the fish sauce and verjuice for 1 minute. Add the prepared asian stock, crabmeat and roasted tomatoes, and reduce by a third.

Stir through the cooked pasta and serve with a garnish of parsley and coriander leaves.

[serves: 6]

asian stock:

3 tablespoons peanut oil

2 birds' eye chillies, cut in half

2 lemon grass stalks, crushed and cut into four

3 cm piece ginger, peeled and sliced

2 whole star anise

1/4 bunch coriander roots, roughly chopped

1 brown onion, roughly chopped

1 carrot, roughly chopped

2 kaffir lime leaves

8 cups water

recipe : john kennedy & justine matthews : the pass café

" What I like about Byron is that there are black ones and white ones, rich ones and poor ones, gay ones and straight ones, then you throw in some backpackers and it's a really interesting mix of people. **"**

Steve Snow
Fins Restaurant

ingredients:

24 king prawns, cleaned and shelled (leave heads and tails on)

lisbone paste:

3 red capsicums

2 cloves garlic, chopped

sea salt

1/2 cup olive oil

basting oil:

100 gm butter

100 ml olive oil

2 cloves garlic, chopped

1 tablespoon lemon rind, grated

1 teaspoon thyme

risotto:

100 ml olive oil

1 onion, sliced

2 cloves garlic, chopped

250 gm arborio rice

250 ml beetroot juice

250 ml pinot noir (red wine)

1 litre fish or chicken stock

1 bay leaf

2 tablespoons parsley, chopped

salt and pepper

1 tablespoon butter

mayonnaise:

2 egg yolks

1 tablespoon mustard

1/4 teaspoon saffron powder

1 tablespoon white wine vinegar

salt and pepper

1 cup vegetable oil

1 tablespoon hot water

char-grilled prawns with beetroot and pinot risotto and saffron mayonnaise

To make the lisbone paste, cut the capsicums in half and char over a flame, then remove the skin and seeds. Blend the capsicum, garlic and a pinch of salt in a food processor. With the motor running, slowly add the olive oil to form a paste. Marinate the prawns in the lisbone paste for 10 minutes.

For the basting oil, combine the butter, olive oil, garlic, lemon rind and thyme.

Char-grill the marinated prawns on a hot grill, brushing occasionally with the basting oil.

To make the risotto, heat the olive oil in a large pan. Add onion and garlic and cook for 1 minute, then add arborio rice and stir through. Slowly start to add the beetroot juice, pinot noir, and the stock, a little at a time. Add the bay leaf and the parsley, then season with salt and pepper. When the rice is cooked, stir in the butter, and remove the bay leaf.

To make the mayonnaise, place the egg yolks, mustard, saffron, vinegar, salt and pepper in a blender. Combine, and then slowly add the vegetable oil in a steady stream, until it thickens, and then add the hot water.

To serve, place the char-grilled prawns on top of the risotto and serve with the saffron mayonnaise.

[serves: 6]

recipe : steve snow : fins restaurant

ingredients:

100 ml olive oil

6 cloves garlic, finely chopped

1 red onion, finely chopped

430 ml water

sea salt

220 gm polenta

10 fresh oregano leaves, finely sliced

4 medium flat mushrooms, stems removed

1 clove garlic, finely sliced

100 ml olive oil, extra

juice of 1 lemon

400 gm english spinach, washed

sea salt

cracked pepper

200 gm goats cheese

crispy polenta with mushrooms, wilted spinach and goats cheese

To make polenta, heat olive oil in a deep pot. Sauté garlic and onion over moderate heat, stirring for 5 minutes. Add water, bring to the boil. Add salt, then simmer, gradually pouring in polenta, whisking constantly. Continue to stir over low heat for 10 minutes. Fold oregano through polenta, then spread polenta into a greased baking dish. Leave to cool. Cut polenta into triangles, brush with a little olive oil, place on a baking tray in a preheated 220°C oven for 20 minutes until golden.

Place mushrooms, open side up, on a greased oven tray. Place sliced garlic over mushrooms, then drizzle with half olive oil and lemon juice. Season with salt and pepper. Place in a preheated 220°C oven for 10 minutes until soft in the centre.

Heat remaining olive oil in a pan, then toss spinach leaves for 2 minutes, being careful not to burn. Add salt and pepper.

To serve, place 2 polenta wedges in centre of plate, place mushrooms and wilted spinach on top, then add goats cheese, cracked pepper and sea salt.

[serves: 4]

recipe : john kennedy & justine matthews : the pass café

The ocean lapping the "great arc" that is the Bay, gave the new settlers both transport and food from the earliest days. With the first long ocean jetty opening in 1888, the little town became a thriving port, coastal steamers collecting goods and passengers, and a fishing fleet operating until the disastrous 1954 cyclone. The last of the jetties, so popular with children and fishermen, was demolished in the early seventies.

The surfers chasing the "endless summer" of the sixties brought with them tastes acquired in their world-travelling, and by the early seventies the Byron food scene was offering much more than most country towns. Mexican Mick's was established in 1969, to the bemusement of many locals, who couldn't imagine why the town needed a restaurant, and it was joined by others offering exotica such as pizzas, teriyaki soy burgers and wheatgerm smoothies. The Aquarius Festival in 1973 in nearby Nimbin encouraged the alternative lifestyle movement, and vegetarian items on menus became more than side-salads. By the mid-eighties, Byron Bay was marked on the international backpacking map and property prices climbed rapidly as escapees from the city saw opportunities. The old industries of whaling, meatworks, sandmining and the Norco factory had gone. Tourism was the new mantra, and there were many chanting its praise.

crocodile and smoked salmon
on lemon myrtle noodles and ginger cream sauce

To make the noodles, place the flour, semolina, eggs, lemon myrtle and salt into a bowl and mix until smooth and a dough is formed. Refrigerate for 2 hours, then roll out and cut into noodles with a pasta machine. Blanch in hot water for 2 minutes, then refresh in cold water.

To make the sauce, place the ginger, garlic, coriander, mustard and chilli in a blender and process until combined. With the motor running, slowly add the oil in a steady stream.

Sauté the crocodile in a hot pan with a small amount of olive oil until partially cooked. Stir in the ginger sauce and bring to the boil. Add the cream, bring back to the boil, remove from the heat and add the smoked salmon.

To serve, reheat the noodles and top with crocodile and salmon mixture.

[serves: 6]

recipe : greg mcburney : the raving prawn

ingredients:

500 gm crocodile, cut into 1 cm dice

1/4 cup olive oil

500 gm smoked salmon, cut into 1 1/2 cm strips

noodles:

150 gm plain flour

75 gm semolina

2 whole eggs

6 lemon myrtle leaves, finely chopped

salt

sauce:

2 cm piece ginger, peeled and sliced

2 cloves garlic, crushed

1/4 bunch coriander

2 tablespoons dijon mustard

1 chilli, chopped

200 ml vegetable oil

100 ml cream

❝ There's something about Byron – its nature and beauty – energy from the sea, the rainforest, the dolphins – even the individuals who come with love and peace in their hearts.

I'm not certain, but I have watched the faces of some toughs and the moment they step off their motorbikes and stroll down to the water – stand there with their hands in their pockets, looking out to sea – a transformation occurs – they become almost peaceful gentle giants.

The spirit of the seventies is truly alive in Byron. "

Victoria Thompson
author

ingredients:	quince:
500 ml cream	1 cup castor sugar
150 gm sugar	1 cup water
1/2 lemon zest	6 quince, peeled and sliced
2 tablespoons honey	toffee wafers:
1 vanilla bean, split	90 gm castor sugar
4 gelatine sheets	100 ml golden syrup
400 ml boiling water	100 gm butter
600 ml plain yoghurt	90 gm flour

honey bavarois with poached quince and toffee wafer

In a saucepan, combine 150 ml of cream, sugar, zest, honey and split vanilla bean. Bring to the boil, then remove from the heat. Soak the gelatine sheets in boiling water, remove, and add the gelatine to the cream mixture. Return the saucepan to the heat, until the gelatine has dissolved, then strain. Lightly whip the remaining cream and yoghurt, and then combine the two cream mixtures. Pour the mixture into lightly greased dariole moulds, and refrigerate until set.

To poach the quince, heat the sugar and water in a saucepan until the sugar dissolves, then add the quince. Poach until the quince is tender.

To make the toffee wafers, melt the sugar, syrup and butter in a saucepan, then fold through the flour. Spoon the toffee mixture (a teaspoon size each) onto a greased oven tray, and bake in a 180°C oven until golden.

To serve, use a sharp knife to carefully loosen each bavarois from the edge of each mould and turn out onto serving plates. Rest a toffee wafer on the side of each bavarois and serve with the poached quince.

[serves: 6]

recipe : steve snow : fins restaurant

ingredients:

4 sheets filo pastry

50 gm unsalted butter, melted

25 gm ground cinnamon

75 gm castor sugar

1 punnet blueberries

1 punnet raspberries

1 punnet blackberries

200 ml cream

125 gm mascarpone

2 tablespoons castor sugar

forest berry tart

Lightly brush all the sheets of filo pastry with melted butter, and sprinkle with the combined cinnamon and sugar. Lay the sheets one on top of the other, and cut into 6 pieces. Place into individual greased pie tins and bake in a 220°C oven for 5 minutes. Remove pastry from the tins and let cool.

Combine the 3 punnets of berries and spoon into the pastry cases. Whip the cream, mascarpone and castor sugar until stiff peaks are formed, and then dollop the cream mixture onto the berry tarts and serve.

[serves: 6]

recipe : greg mcburney : the raving prawn

café

In what other town would
the updated counts of
local election results be
posted on blackboards
outside cafés? In what
other area would the
frothing quality of the
milk for cappuccinos be
debated on page two of
the daily paper? Where
else are stories of giving
up caffeine, and falls
from the "wagon",
discussed in hushed
and serious voices?

An "LSD" (latté-soy-dandy) just isn't the same for some.

Cafés proliferate and keep the wheels turning on everything from local politics to love affairs, while providing some great coffees, great meals and a great place to simply sit and watch the brave new world go by.

sticky black rice with coconut cream and papaya

ingredients:

1 1/2 cups indonesian black rice

750 ml water

1 small pandanus leaf

150 gm shaved palm sugar

1 cinnamon stick

3 cm knob ginger, sliced

250 ml coconut cream

1 ripe papaya or mango

Place well-rinsed rice in a bowl, cover with water and leave to stand overnight.

Put soaked rice and water in a pan, bring to the boil over medium heat, adding pandanus leaf, palm

sugar, cinnamon stick and ginger. Gently simmer until water is almost absorbed and the rice develops

a creamy consistency. Remove pandanus leaf, cinnamon stick and allow rice to thoroughly cool.

Peel and seed papaya and cut into wide sections.

Place rice into bowls, top with sliced papaya and surround with coconut cream.

[serves: 4]

recipe : john bassett : café viva

Byron is the kind of town that recognises the importance of a really good breakfast, even if you are having it in the afternoon. Locals have their favourite town haunts for an after-early-morning-swim fruit salad or a pre-work bacon and egg special, and the Beach Café is where everyone goes when they want a sunny beach-side setting, and the Pass Café for rainforest-sheltered privacy. There are cafés and restaurants to be found around town wherever there are shops, another safety feature for anyone likely to be feeling exhausted after a heavy round of retail therapy.

If you want to pack your own picnic, you can even make it all organic with produce from the many different specialist shops. If you choose a supermarket, you will always have to move around a group of golden-tanned backpackers debating seriously in German/Swedish/Japanese/French. No translation is required, they are always calculating whether the combined budget will stretch to an expensive ice-cream for dessert.

"Then, he clasps each of them in turn in the **Byron squeeze.** This is a lengthy bear hug executed with closed eyes, wide smiles and lots of sideways rocking, hair stroking optional, which can be performed, so far as I can tell, anyway, whether the huggers have been apart for years or one has simply gone up the road for a peppermint tea earlier in the day."

From 'Sartori', by Linda Jaivin
author

ingredients:

750 gm pumpkin	salt and pepper
750 gm sweet potato	1/2 cup white wine
1 clove garlic, minced	2 cups thickened cream
1 brown onion, finely diced	1 cup parmesan cheese, ext
3/4 cup parmesan cheese	6 roma tomatoes
1/4 bunch parsley, finely chopped	1/2 cup olive oil
3/4 cup semolina	1 bunch rocket
4 eggs	1/2 bunch chives

baked sweet potato and pumpkin gnocchi and parmesan cream sauce

Peel and roughly chop the pumpkin and sweet potato. Place into a saucepan, cover with water and bring to the boil. Cook for approximately 20 minutes until the pumpkin and potatoes are very tender. Strain and place into a large mixing bowl, mash and allow to cool. Combine the garlic, onion, parmesan cheese, parsley, semolina, eggs, salt and pepper, with the mashed vegetables. Mix well and then pour the mixture into a greased and lined baking tray. Place into a preheated 200°C oven for approximately 40 minutes, or until firm. Remove from the oven and allow to cool. Remove the baked gnocchi from the tray and cut into triangular pieces. Grill each piece on all sides until golden brown.

To make the sauce, place the wine into a saucepan, and cook over medium heat until it has reduced by half. Add the cream and simmer for 10 minutes. Whisk until the cream mixture thickens, and then stir in the parmesan cheese, salt and pepper.

Cut the roma tomatoes in half lengthwise, drizzle with the olive oil and season with salt and pepper. Place on a baking tray and roast in a preheated 220°C oven for approximately 15 minutes.

To serve, place a few rocket leaves on a plate and drizzle with olive oil. Place 2 slices of gnocchi on top of the leaves, with the roasted tomatoes on the side. Pour the cream sauce over the top and garnish with the chives.

[serves: 4]

recipe : danielle laurie : fresh

"People come to Byron for its special flavour. What you see, feel and smell as you are eating here adds up to the actual real taste, the one that lasts longer than the meal. Atmosphere and context is essential to the art of savouring taste. For the maximum pleasure in tasting Byron food we recommend that one should earn the appetite with a good walk, run, golf game or perhaps a couple of miles paddling a surfboard through the waves. Here, we the blessed lifestylers like to do an endeavour, say a prayer for others less fortunate and then launch into our dishes with purpose and sufficient appetite for the world."

Rusty Miller
former U.S. surfing champion

the BYRON routine
1 SURF
2 Breakfast
3. SURF
4 coffee
5. surf
6 LUNCH
7 SNoozzzzze
8 SURF
9 AT LAST IT'S
PIZZA TIME

Surfers often resort to spiritual images to describe the particular addiction that the ocean holds for devotees. "Better than sex" is sometimes claimed, and given the amount of time and energy that surfers expend on their boards, this may be true for some! The first visiting surfers camped in their panel vans and station-wagons screened with home-sewn curtains, wolfing down fish and chips with a pint of Norco's finest chocolate milk when a meal was necessary. Many who came for the surf, stayed to run a business and raise a family, and surfing is still a part of their lives. Just check the line up of tradesmen's vans with empty board-racks at the beach when the surf is pumping…

ingredients:

8 kransky sausages

mash:

4 cloves garlic

4 tablespoons olive oil

4 large desiree potatoes, peeled and diced

75 gm butter

1 tablespoon dijon mustard

1/2 cup milk

salsa verde:

1 slice stale or toasted sourdough bread

1 hard boiled egg

1 cup extra virgin olive oil

1/2 lemon, juiced

2 cups parsley, chopped

5 basil leaves, chopped

1 clove garlic

1 tablespoon capers

1 tablespoon grated parmesan cheese

salt and pepper

kransky sausages on roast garlic mash with salsa verde

Char-grill the kransky sausages, keep warm and put aside until needed.

To prepare the garlic mash, place garlic cloves on a flat tray and cover with olive oil. Roast in a hot oven until golden brown and tender. Boil potatoes in salty water until soft. While potatoes are still hot, place into a food processor with the roasted garlic, butter and mustard. Turn the food processor onto low speed and gradually add milk until mixture is smooth, but not runny.

To make the salsa verde, combine all the ingredients in a food processor and pulse until mixture has a thick consistency. Salsa verde can be stored in a container with a film of olive oil over the top to preserve. Cover with a lid and store refrigerated, until required.

Place mash in the centre of 4 plates. Cut sausages on the diagonal and arrange on top of the mash. Spoon a generous amount of salsa verde on top of the sausages and serve.

[serves: 4]

recipe : kyle hughes : the rails bistro

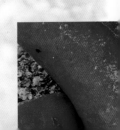

" In Byron Bay the parking police have a practice of chalking the wheel of your car when you park in Jonson Street. This ensures that any motorist who has parked longer than the prescribed hour will be fined.

A more appropriate practice would be to adopt this procedure in Byron cafés. A café patrol officer would rove these much-frequented establishments and chalk the legs of the coffee shop patrons.

Anyone found sitting more than one hour would be fined,

those who refuse to move on will have their cappuccinos clamped.

We live by the sea; for god's sake get out of the coffee shop and go to the beach! 🙶

Mandy Nolan
stand-up comic and visual artist who has spent too much productive time lolling over a latté!

ingredients:

12 chicken tenderloins

8 roma tomatoes, cut in half lengthwise

sea salt

cracked black pepper

4 teaspoons pesto sauce

3 tablespoons olive oil

1/2 cup balsamic vinegar

1 bunch rocket leaves, stems removed

dressing:

2 tablespoons olive oil

2 tablespoons balsamic vinegar

cornbread:

1/3 cup safflower oil

2 eggs, lightly beaten

3/4 cup creamed corn

1/2 cup sour cream

1 small onion, chopped

3/4 cup polenta

1 teaspoon baking powder

1 tablespoon coriander, chopped

1 red chilli, seeded and chopped

sea salt

1/2 cup light cheddar cheese, grated

guacamole:

3 avocados

1 clove garlic, crushed

1 teaspoon sweet chilli sauce

2 dashes tabasco sauce

1/2 lemon, juiced

1 tablespoon coriander, chopped

1/4 cup sour cream

balsamic chicken with cornbread, roasted tomatoes and guacamole

To make cornbread, preheat oven to 180°C and line a small 3 cm deep baking tray with baking paper. Combine safflower oil, eggs, creamed corn, sour cream and onion. Then combine polenta, baking powder, coriander, chilli and salt. Mix all this together then spread half the mixture over the base of the lined baking tray. Sprinkle with the grated cheese and spread the remaining mixture over the top. Bake for 60 minutes. Remove from the oven and allow to cool in the baking tray.

While cornbread is cooking, brush the roma tomatoes with pesto sauce, sprinkle with salt, pepper and olive oil. Roast in 180°C oven for 30 minutes.

To prepare the guacamole, mash the avocados, add the garlic, sweet chilli sauce, tabasco sauce, lemon juice and coriander. Fold through the sour cream.

Season chicken tenderloins with salt and pepper. Heat a non-stick pan. Brown both sides of the chicken tenderloins in a little olive oil, then add balsamic vinegar. Reduce liquid over high heat until chicken tenderloins are cooked and slightly caramelised.

To assemble, cut cornbread into eight triangles. Place two pieces of warm cornbread on a plate, resting one upon the other. Place tomatoes and a spoonful of guacamole on the side of the cornbread and the chicken on top of the cornbread. Top the dish with a few rocket leaves, dressed in the balsamic vinegar and olive oil.

[serves: 4]

recipe : john bassett : café viva

Don't go looking for big-name takeaways for snack attacks, Byron Bay is a Mac-free zone and aiming to stay that way. Development of the town is a contentious issue, with all opinions fulsomely expressed. Mayor of the Byron Shire Council is Tom Wilson, currently owner of the Byronian Café, formerly a major in the SAS, who typifies the diversity of experience which makes the community both rich and sometimes volatile.

"Our community is passionate about the natural things that make it such a special place to live, and keeping it local and low-key is part of our success formula. This is reflected in our restaurants and cafés as much as it is in our view of local politics, the environment and the richness of our community. May it stay as unpretentious as it is."

Tom Wilson
mayor

mocha indulgence

Combine all the ingredients, except the chocolate and strawberries, in a blender.
Blend until smooth and pour into chilled glasses. To serve, sprinkle shaved
chocolate over the top and garnish with a strawberry if desired.

[serves: 4]

recipe : franco ivancich : byron bay coffee company

ingredients:

1 1/2 cups double-strength
plunger coffee, chilled

1/2 cup milk

1/3 cup cream

1 cup chocolate ice-cream

120 ml kahlua

80 ml brandy

80 gm shaved dark chocolate

4 strawberries (optional)

"Why get off at Redfern when you can go all the way to Byron Bay?" asks the sign at the Railway Friendly Bar. Indeed, if you have to return to Redfern or further afield, you can await the train's arrival with an ale or even a meal from the Rails Bistro. The opening of the railway in 1894 brought the possibilities of amazingly rapid transport for people and goods, where previously arduous journeys through rough country or rougher seas were the only option.

Originally "refreshment rooms" for "bona fide travellers", the Rails is now known world-wide as a friendly place where locals, backpackers and tourists meet for a drink, a meal and some music. Stand-up poets declaim one Sunday afternoon each month, and any visiting national or international poet is likely to find him or herself reading under the tin roof as other poets, dreamers, drinkers and passing tourists apportion approximately the same attention as for familiar local bards. Many of the original streets in Byron Bay are named after poets, due to an early misconception over the naming of the Cape!

balinese beef curry

Combine all the bali spice paste ingredients in a food processor, and blend until coarsely ground.

Cook over medium heat, in a heavy-based frypan, until golden brown.

In a large pot, place the bali spice paste and half the coconut milk. Stir over medium heat until mixture is combined and has a creamy texture. Place the beef and the remaining coconut milk in the pot, and add enough water (400 ml) to cover the meat. Place a bruised stem of lemon grass into the pot. Bring to the boil, then reduce heat. Cover the pot and simmer until beef is very tender.

Season with salt, lime juice and kecap manis.

Place the washed rice and the saffron threads into a large saucepan. Cover with enough water (400 ml) to bring the level to 2 cm above the rice and stir. Bring to the boil, then reduce heat and simmer with a lid on for approximately 5 minutes until the rice is cooked. Serve with the curry.

[serves: 4]

recipe : kyle hughes : the rails bistro

ingredients:

800 ml coconut milk

600 gm chuck steak, cubed

800 ml water

1 stick lemon grass

salt

2 limes, juiced

1 tablespoon kecap manis (sweet soy)

2 cups long-grain rice

10 saffron threads

bali spice paste:

3 red onions

6 cloves garlic

5 cm peeled ginger

10 cm piece peeled galangal

6 large red chillies

7 birds' eye chillies

10 candlenuts or macadamia nuts

1 tablespoon freshly ground coriander seeds

1 tablespoon freshly ground black peppercorns

4 tablespoons peanut oil

"Byron Bay. The hugging/massage/feral/alternative/pose 'n' passion capital of Oz. That's its image, anyhow. But there is another more serious possibility: **is Byron the nation's first successful attempt at a sophisticated urban culture outside our cities?"**

Craig McGregor
writer, journalist

" Coffee is not a drink.
Cola is a drink.
Coffee is a work of art."

Gary Trye
coffee presenter and educator

country

The earth and sea around Byron Bay was always rich with food, and the bushfood industry is just discovering the natural resources of the land. Macadamias, the original bushfood, originated in this region, but have only developed as a local industry decades after Hawaii exploited their potential. Our newly developing coffee industry is a reincarnation of the industry early last century, and the rich volcanic soils produce a very clean, high quality bean which is just being discovered internationally. The sheer variety of produce now farmed is inspiring a new regional cuisine, marked by an emphasis on fresh, seasonal, organic and simply prepared foods, with excellent seafood and vegetarian options.

regional farming:

asian vegetables

avocados

bamboo

bananas

beef

blueberries

bushfoods

chillies

citrus

coffee

custard apples

dairy

davidson's plum

dragonfruit

finger limes

herbs

lemon myrtle

limes

lychees

macadamias

mangos

olives

organic vegetables

ostrich farming

oyster mushrooms

papaya

passionfruit

pork

seafood

soybeans

stone fruit

sugar

sweet potatoes

tamarinds

tea

ingredients:

300 gm atlantic salmon fillet, boned and skinned

salt and pepper

12 squid tubes, cleaned

12 large basil leaves

1 tablespoon kecap manis (sweet soy)

1 tablespoon olive oil

50 gm clarified butter

1/2 bunch rocket, chopped

1/2 bunch rocket, extra

lime wedges

pink peppercorns, cracked

capsicum coulis:

2 large red capsicums, roasted and peeled

1/4 small red onion, chopped

2 cloves garlic, crushed

1 teaspoon spanish paprika

1 teaspoon dill, chopped

1 teaspoon extra virgin olive oil

1 teaspoon tarragon vinegar

30 ml mirin

salt and pepper

buttermilk dressing:

50 ml buttermilk

10 ml davidson's plum syrup

1/2 lime, juiced

atlantic salmon and basil stuffed squid with roasted capsicum coulis and burnt rocket butter

For the capsicum coulis, place all the ingredients into a food processor, and blend until smooth.

Season the salmon fillet with salt and pepper, and cut it into 12 pieces, just big enough to fit into the squid. Roll each piece of salmon in a basil leaf, and insert these into the squid (smallest end first). Secure the opening with a toothpick, then marinate the squid in the kecap manis. Heat the olive oil in a heavy-based pan, and sear the squid on all sides, for approximately 4 minutes, until brown. Remove the toothpicks and keep warm.

Heat the clarified butter in the hot pan, and toss in the rocket, heat through, remove and keep warm.

To make the buttermilk dressing, combine the buttermilk, davidson's plum syrup and the lime juice, refrigerate until serving time.

To serve, slice the squid in half on the diagonal, spoon the coulis onto the centre of a plate, drizzle the rocket butter and the dressing around the edge. Lay fresh rocket leaves on the coulis, and then the cut squid. Serve with a sprinkling of pink pepper and lime wedges.

[serves: 6]

recipe : shaun white : wild about food

> " The challenge being met in this area is to create edible landscapes in harmony with our natural environment. To be Green is to seek to live lightly on the land, enhance it, revel in it and produce food fit for the gods but accessible to all. "

Ian Cohen
Byron Bay conservationist
NSW Green Member of Parliament

Originally lowland sub-tropical rainforest, or the "Big Scrub", covered the whole of this region. Place names such as Possum Shoot and Coopers Shoot mark the areas where the huge logs slid down the hills for collection and transport by bullock team to the mills. When the timber-fellers finished cutting down the magnificent red cedar and hoop pines at the end of the nineteenth century, the remaining trees were cleared and burnt to open up the land for farming. Clearing of land was usually a condition of selection, and early photographs show rural scenes which appear as wholesale devastation to our eyes, yet to most of the pioneers was progress, though some decried the waste of timber.

Green politics developed out of the protests against logging and dams in the seventies, and the fight to save the remnants of our natural heritage continues. Eco-tourism is the future, with our unique rainforest, beaches and countryside having a special magic, where today so much is concrete, and so many places have lost their individuality to global commerce. A walk through the rainforest to one of the beaches at Broken Head shows how this whole coastline looked just a century ago.

ingredients:

4 red onions

4 tablespoons salt

1 1/2 cups white vinegar

3/4 cup castor sugar

1 fresh bay leaf

optional ingredients:

2 cm piece ginger, julienned

1 red chilli, julienned

sliced pickled onions

Slice the onions and put into a stainless steel bowl and mix with salt.

Leave for 1 hour, rinse off the salt and drain well. Bring the vinegar,

sugar, bay leaf, ginger and chilli (if using), to the boil and pour over the

onions. Cool for 4 hours, then place into sterilised jars.

[serves: makes 2 cups]

recipe : wendy taylor : byron bay cooking school

Many lonely old farmhouses, forgotten school-masters' cottages and other often almost derelict country buildings have found a whole new life as bed and breakfast establishments. New hosts talk cheerfully of the excitement of discovering the building, the hard work of evicting feral goats from the living room and rebuilding whole sections which simply collapsed when the termites stopped holding hands. Others find their dream location and build houses big enough to share. Such gregarious hosts find the pleasure of entertaining new people outweighs the hard work of being on call around the clock and cooking elaborate breakfasts each morning, regardless of the night before. Some bed and breakfasts operate like boutique hotels, offering changing menus to in-house guests for dinners, picnics and barbecues, and drawing guests on their culinary reputation as well as their setting.

ingredients:

8 free range eggs

1 tablespoon vinegar

3/4 cup plain flour

2 beaten eggs

2 cups fresh breadcrumbs

1/2 cup oil for frying

salt

crunchy eggs

To poach the eggs, add vinegar to a pot of water and bring to the boil. Have the eggs ready to tip into the pot by breaking onto a couple of saucers. Take the pot off the heat and gently tip in the eggs. Cover and leave for 3-4 minutes until the whites are cooked. Use a slotted spoon to remove the eggs, then place them in a bowl of cold water until ready to use.

Trim the poached eggs of any straggly pieces and pat dry. Carefully dip the eggs into the flour seasoned with salt, then into the beaten eggs and finally pat on the breadcrumbs. Heat 1/2 cm of oil in a heavy-based frypan, gently cook the eggs until golden, then turn and cook the other side. Drain on kitchen paper.

Serve with steamed asparagus, tomato salsa, puréed spinach or char-grilled zucchini.

[serves: 4]

recipe : wendy taylor : byron bay cooking school

The angular peak of Mt Warning dominates the skyline around much of the far north coast of New South Wales. The plug of a long-extinct volcano, it is a stunning place to see the dawn. The rich soil which drew the farmers to clear so much of the land owes its origins to this explosive ancient history.

Today, some landowners are regenerating the rainforest, creating wildlife corridors. Many of the original dairy farms have been consolidated and diversified, others have become the hobby farms and rural retreats of families enjoying the slower pace of country life. New settlers migrate not just from across the country, but from across the world.

" People often ask me why I moved from a flourishing life in New York City to the hinterland of Byron Bay. I tell them it's because I am very lucky and very smart. "

Alison Pearl
writer, music promoter

ingredients:

2 brown onions, finely diced

450 ml dry white wine

125 ml white wine vinegar

4 lemon myrtle leaves

250 gm unsalted butter,
chopped and chilled

salt and pepper

100 ml olive oil

1 clove garlic, finely chopped

1/2 bulb fennel, finely diced

1 teaspoon fennel seeds, roasted

1/2 preserved lime, finely chopped

250 gm arborio rice

750 ml fish stock

4 salmon fillets, skin on

1 tablespoon sugar

100 ml water

1/2 red capsicum

5 cm piece ginger, peeled

1 bunch bok choy

crisp-skin tasmanian salmon with preserved lime and fennel risotto and lemon myrtle beurre blanc

Place half the onion, 200 ml white wine, vinegar and the lemon myrtle leaves in a saucepan over medium heat and reduce to a jam-like consistency. Place the mixture in a bowl over a saucepan of simmering water, and gradually whisk in the cold butter, piece by piece. Continue to whisk until thickened, season with salt and pepper, then remove the lemon myrtle leaves. Keep the beurre blanc warm until needed.

Heat some olive oil in a heavy-based saucepan. Add the remaining onion, garlic, chopped fennel bulb and stir until softened. Stir in the fennel seeds, preserved lime and the rice, and continue stirring for about 3 minutes. Simmer the stock, then slowly add it to the rice with the remaining white wine, about 100 ml at a time, stirring constantly for 20 minutes until the rice has absorbed all the liquid and is cooked. When cooled, roll into balls, heat a little olive oil in a pan and lightly brown the risotto cakes.

Heat the remaining olive oil in a heavy-based pan. Score a diamond pattern on the skin of the salmon. Sear the salmon, skin side down, for approximately 2-3 minutes, turn over and cook for a further 2-3 minutes on the other side.

Heat the sugar and water over medium heat. Cut the capsicum and ginger into thin strips and cook in the sugar and water syrup until softened.

To serve, steam the bok choy and place on a plate. Place a risotto cake and then a salmon fillet on the bok choy. Twist the capsicum and ginger, place on the top of the salmon fillet and surround with the lemon myrtle beurre blanc.

[serves: 4]

recipe : robert fleming : byron's roving chef

In the late sixties, the flower children who couldn't afford a ticket to San Francisco moved to the far north coast of New South Wales. Casting aside their former suburban incarnations, they grew vegetables, made chunky pottery and rainbow-coloured candles, did leatherwork and set tofu, all of which they sold at markets they founded.

Ironically, many of the children of the region who'd grown up in families where vegie gardens, handsewn and knitted clothes and fish caught for dinner were simply a way of surviving, migrated to the cities, bemused that others would find growing their own food amazing. (A lot of them have returned.) New arrivals set up cafés and restaurants which drew more visitors and more settlers. Where Ryan's Café and Hall's fish and chip shop had sufficed for decades, diversity had arrived and thrived.

The markets flourished and are a fascinating place to find unusual hand crafts, original clothing, get a tarot reading or a massage, listen to the buskers and enjoy a real lemonade, a vegetarian spring roll with plum sauce or a coffee and baklava.

rainbow-peppered scallops with squid ink linguine and prawn butter

Brush capsicum with olive oil and season with salt and pepper. Roast capsicum in a hot oven until well cooked. When cooled, remove skin, seeds and slice into thin strips. Put aside.

Heat 80 gm of the butter in a saucepan. Cook onions, galangal and prawn shells on high heat, until onion is transparent. Add white wine, seafood stock and kaffir lime leaves, then reduce by half and strain.

Boil 2 litres of water in a large pot. Add linguine, cook until al dente, then drain.

Sprinkle scallops with freshly ground rainbow peppercorns and sea salt. In a very hot pan, quickly sear scallops, seasoned side down, then turn over, season and sear other side and remove from the pan. While the pan is still hot, add sliced roasted capsicum, prawn sauce and remaining 40 gm butter.

Arrange the heated linguine on a plate, top with the scallops and pour over the prawn sauce.

[serves: 4]

recipe : darren bridge : wild about food

92

ingredients:

300 gm squid ink linguine

2 litres water

20 large roe on sea scallops

1 tablespoon rainbow peppercorns
(mixture of black, white, green, red
and pink peppercorns)

sea salt

sauce:

2 red capsicums

1 tablespoon olive oil

salt and pepper

120 gm butter

2 onions, finely diced

2 teaspoons galangal, grated

12 prawns, shells and heads only
(prawn meat not needed)

30 ml white wine

400 ml seafood or fish stock

4 kaffir lime leaves

Hinterland villages such as Bangalow, ten minutes west of Byron Bay, have been rediscovered over the last decade and the quaint old buildings which survived because no one wanted to invest in the town in the era of big, chunky supermarkets are now stylishly renovated restaurants and galleries. Larger towns such as Mullumbimby and Brunswick Heads have also changed from sleepy service centres for local farmers to diverse and vibrant communities as hippies, yuppies, artists, musicians and city escapees moved in with new attitudes, ideas, money and businesses. Some residents are fortunate enough to be able to enjoy the country lifestyle while telecommuting, others open new practices or start local industries. "It's not a career move, it's a lifestyle move," is the saying.

ingredients:

2 free range chickens (size 10)

1 head garlic

1 tablespoon olive oil

2 jumbo quails (200 gm)

1 lemon, grated

1 orange, grated

80 gm pistachio nuts, peeled

1/2 bunch continental parsley, finely chopped

1/2 bunch basil, finely chopped

white pepper, freshly ground

sea salt

to serve:

spicy relish

1 loaf sourdough bread, sliced

chicken and quail terrine with
roasted garlic, pistachio and fresh herbs

Remove the skin from the chickens in one piece, by cutting the skin along

the backbone, and gently lifting the skin away from the flesh, being careful

not to tear it. Grease a 1.5 litre ovenproof terrine dish, and then line it with

2 layers of tin foil. Line the terrine dish with the chicken skin. Wrap the garlic

and the olive oil in foil, and roast in the oven for 20 minutes. Remove the

flesh from the chicken and the quail, discarding the quail skin. Cut the

chicken and quail meat into 1 cm strips. In a bowl, mix together the meat,

grated lemon rind, orange rind, pistachio nuts, peeled roasted garlic,

parsley, basil, salt and pepper. Place the mixture into the skin-lined terrine

dish, pressing down well. Fold the skin over the top to enclose, and trim off

any excess. Cover with 2 layers of greased foil and a lid. Place the terrine

into a baking dish and half fill the dish with hot water. Cook in a preheated

170°C oven for approximately 1 hour, until the centre is hot when tested

with a metal skewer. Remove from the oven and allow to cool. Place a

weight on the top of the terrine and refrigerate overnight.

To serve, dip the terrine into hot water for about 1 minute and turn onto a cutting board. Using

a hot, dry knife cut into 1 cm slices and serve with a spicy relish and toasted sourdough bread.

[serves: 12]

recipe : michael de laurence : taylor's country house

"I like to party, I like entertaining. With a bed and breakfast you get paid to do that!

It took a lot of effort to get Taylor's approved and we opened in the mid-eighties and sold it in the mid-nineties. You get to meet the most fascinating people, the famous, the infamous, the exotic and the flagrantly erotic, everyone from petty crooks to politicians. And what's more, it's tax-deductible! **"**

Wendy Taylor
Byron Bay Cooking School
B&B expert and advisor

tamarillo and cinnamon biscuit wafers

Place wine, water, sugar, cinnamon sticks and peppercorns into a large pot. Bring to the boil, then simmer for 5 minutes. Cut a small cross in the end of each tamarillo, and place into the red wine syrup. Bring back to the boil, then remove from heat and cover. When cooled, remove tamarillos from pot, and slide off the skins. Put fruit aside. Replace pot over low heat and reduce the syrup by a third, then strain and cool.

To make the biscuit wafers, mix sugar and cinnamon together. Brush a sheet of filo pastry with melted butter. Sprinkle pastry with half the sugar mix. Cut pastry into 4 strips approximately 10 cm x 28 cm. Fold the long side in half to measure approximately 5 cm wide, then fold into thirds to form a neat wafer. Repeat process with remaining pastry and sugar mix until 8 wafers have been made. Place pastry onto a lightly greased oven tray and bake at 180°C for 7 minutes or until crisp and golden.

To assemble, keep 4 whole tamarillos to serve. Slice remaining fruit into thin slices. Place a few slices in the centre of each plate, then top with a wafer and neatly arrange more fruit on the wafer. Top with another wafer then dust with icing sugar. Place a whole tamarillo on the side, drizzle reduced syrup around plate and serve with a dollop of yoghurt.

[serves: 4]

recipe : wendy taylor : byron bay cooking school

ingredients:

1 cup red wine

1 cup water

2 cups castor sugar

2 cinnamon sticks

1 tablespoon peppercorns

12 tamarillos

200 gm thick yoghurt

sprinkling of icing sugar

biscuit wafers:

1 cup castor sugar

2 cinnamon sticks, freshly ground

2 sheets filo pastry

50 gm melted butter

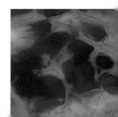

Along with the alternate lifestyles of many of the
new settlers came alternate beliefs, alternate
medicines and alternate therapies. Influences
from Asia, with Buddhist and Zen philosophies
melded with a multiplicity of creeds from right across
India and cults from around the world. Acupuncture and massage, iridology and kinesiology,
vegetarian, vegan and macrobiotic diets, tai chi, yoga and meditation were all explored.

Tribal beliefs of the **original inhabitants** of this country were studied, along with Native American

practices, while others looked towards ancient pagan and Celtic cultures for spiritual nurturing. New

Christian churches developed alongside the original denominations. Workshops to explain and train

in anything from permaculture gardening to tantric sex are available almost every week. Bush

medicines such as tea tree oil have proven to be commercial successes, and large companies have

developed from individuals who began selling their products at the markets twenty years ago.

ingredients:

125 gm unsalted butter, chilled

250 gm plain flour, sifted

65 gm icing sugar

1 whole egg

1 bunch red rhubarb

1 1/2 cups castor sugar

1 lemon, juiced

100 ml water

300 ml sour cream

1 dessertspoon cinnamon

3 tablespoons brown sugar

rhubarb and sour cream tartlet,
crusted with cinnamon and brown sugar

Combine diced butter, flour and icing sugar in a food processor. Process until the mix resembles breadcrumbs, then add the egg. Remove from the machine, and knead the pastry quickly and lightly. Wrap in plastic and refrigerate for 20 minutes. Roll the pastry out thinly and line small (10 cm) tart tins with removable bases. Prick the bases with a fork, then chill for 1 hour. Bake the tartlets for approximately 8 minutes in a preheated 190°C oven until golden brown.

Cut the washed rhubarb stems into 4 cm lengths. Place the rhubarb, sugar, lemon juice and water into a heavy-based saucepan. Cover with a lid and cook over a moderate heat until the rhubarb is just tender. Remove the rhubarb from the syrup, drain in a sieve over the saucepan for 5 minutes and allow to cool. Reserve syrup.

Place the cooked tartlet cases (in their tins), onto a baking tray. Fill each tartlet with the drained rhubarb. Top with a scoop of sour cream and sprinkle liberally with the combined cinnamon and brown sugar. Place the tartlets under a preheated grill until the sugar caramelises and the cream begins to melt.

Gently remove the tartlets from the tins, and place on plates. Pour the reserved rhubarb syrup around each tartlet and serve immediately.

[serves: 6]

recipe : michael de laurence : taylor's country house

macadamia pie

To make the pastry, place flour, icing sugar and chilled butter into a food processor. Blend until grainy, adding the egg until a soft dough is formed. Roll out onto a floured board until approximately 5 mm thick. Line the base and sides of a greased 25 cm spring form tin with the pastry, then refrigerate until filling is ready.

Dissolve sugar with lime juice in a saucepan over low heat until golden. In another saucepan, bring cream and honey almost to the boil, and slowly add to the sugar mixture, then stir in the macadamia nuts. Allow to cool slightly, then pour into the chilled pie flan. Place into a preheated 180°C oven for 30 minutes until nuts and pastry start to brown. Cool and refrigerate. To serve, cut into 8 wedges and dollop with double cream.

ingredients:

pastry:

2 1/2 cups plain flour

3/4 cup icing sugar

175 gm chilled unsalted butter, chopped

1 whole egg

filling:

1 1/2 cups castor sugar

1 tablespoon lime juice

150 ml cream

1 tablespoon honey

500 gm unsalted macadamia nuts

to serve:

300 ml double cream

[serves: 8]

recipe : victoria mcewen : ewingsdale country guest house

cosmopolitan

❝ When I first came to Byron Bay 37 years ago, it was to design a house on a superb site at Wategos. There were only three other houses in the vicinity then. I looked over the bay to the 'long descending line of hills that dwindle away to Queensland' and I was awe-struck. It was the beginning of a life-long love affair.

Like all love affairs, it has not always been a bed of roses. There are aspects of the place that aggravate – it is a very fickle society – there is so much **diversity** and **contradiction** and **ambiguity** that sometimes it is hard to know whether you belong or not. Even so, every time I break through the banksia forest in front of our house, and look at the generous, serene, glorious bay, **I fall in love all over again – on a daily basis.** "

Ian D. McKay
architect

ingredients:

prawns:

8 green king prawns

1 clove garlic, crushed

1 tablespoon olive oil

salt and pepper

mussels:

10 mussels, in a half shell

1 clove garlic, crushed

1/4 bunch continental
parsley, chopped

1/4 cup white wine

6 shallots, chopped

oysters:

8 oysters in the shell

4 tablespoons salmon roe

4 tablespoons champagne

calamari:

2 hoods calamari,
sliced into 1 cm rings

1 clove garlic, crushed

10 basil leaves

2 chillies, sliced

1/2 lemon, juiced

1/2 cup olive oil

salt and pepper

artichokes:

8 artichokes

1 clove garlic, crushed

1/4 bunch basil

1 cup olive oil

1 lemon, juiced

olives:

200 gm kalamata olives

1 clove garlic, chopped

40 ml balsamic vinegar

40 ml olive oil

20 ml lemon juice

cracked black pepper

tomato salsa:

1 tomato, chopped

1 red onion, chopped

1 tablespoon parsley, chopped

2 tablespoons balsamic vinegar

2 tablespoons olive oil

cracked black pepper

baba ganoush:

3 eggplants, cut in
half and scored

2 cloves garlic

1 tablespoon sweet
chilli sauce

1 tablespoon ground
coriander

1 tablespoon ground cumin

1 lemon, juiced

1/3 cup natural yoghurt

3 tablespoons olive oil

1/2 bunch coriander

salt and pepper

capsicum:

3 red capsicums

2 tablespoons olive oil

salt and pepper

pesto:

see recipe, page 130 & 131

garnish:

50 gm fetta cheese

3 limes, quartered

1/4 bunch parsley leaves

antipasto plate

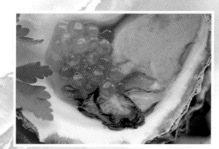

Marinate all the calamari ingredients for 18 hours, prior to use.

Sauté the prawns in a hot pan with garlic, oil, salt and pepper, until they are cooked.

Braise the mussels with the garlic, parsley, white wine and shallots, until cooked through.

Drizzle olive oil over the capsicums and season with salt and pepper. Roast the capsicums in a hot oven until blackened. Remove the skin and seeds, then cut into strips.

Roast the scored eggplants in a hot oven until tender, and scoop out the flesh.
Blend the eggplant with the remaining baba ganoush ingredients, until a paste is formed. Allow all the cooked food to cool.

Combine all the olive ingredients and marinate until needed.

Repeat the process with the artichoke ingredients.

Cut all the salsa ingredients into 1 cm dice, and gently mix together.

Serve the oysters with a splash of champagne and a spoonful of salmon roe,
and the mussels in a half shell, topped with the tomato salsa.

To prepare the antipasto plate, arrange the seafood, olives and artichokes on a platter.
Top off with a spoonful of pesto, roasted capsicum and baba ganoush. Garnish with fetta cheese, parsley and lime wedges.

[serves: 6]

recipe : matthew gillespie : orient restaurant

ingredients:

3 cloves garlic

3 cm piece ginger, peeled and chopped

2 eshallots

3 coriander roots

1/2 teaspoon black peppercorns, ground

1 teaspoon sea salt

1 kg green prawns (reserve shells for sauce)

2 egg whites

1 egg yolk

300 ml cream

250 ml coconut cream

1 tablespoon vegetable oil

sauce:

3 cloves garlic

3 cm piece ginger, peeled and chopped

2 lemon grass stalks, trimmed and sliced

2 eshallots

1 teaspoon black peppercorns, ground

1 kaffir lime, grated (or 8 kaffir lime leaves)

2 large red chillies, seeded

50 ml peanut oil

50 gm palm sugar

75 ml fish sauce

200 ml coconut cream

1 litre water

garnish:

18 large roe on sea scallops

400 gm baby spinach, steamed

1/2 bunch coriander leaves

6 kaffir lime leaves

king prawn mousse cake with scallops and spicy prawn and coconut sauce

Place the garlic, ginger, eshallots, coriander roots, peppercorns and salt in a mortar and pestle,

and pound into a paste. Place the prawn meat and the paste into the bowl of a food processor that

has been chilled in the freezer. With the motor running, add the egg whites one at a time, followed by

the egg yolk and a thin stream of the combined cream and coconut cream. Turn the motor off as

soon as all ingredients are mixed. Spoon the mixture into lightly greased dariole moulds. Place the

moulds into a baking tray and fill the tray with hot water halfway up the sides of the moulds. Cover

the moulds with a sheet of foil, and bake in a preheated 190°C oven for 25 minutes.

To prepare the sauce, pound the garlic, ginger, lemon grass, eshallots, peppercorns, kaffir lime

and chilli into a fine paste. Heat the peanut oil in a heavy-based frying pan. Fry the paste until slightly

coloured, then add the prawn shells, palm sugar, and fish sauce. Caramelise until golden, and then

add the coconut cream and water. Simmer for approximately 25 minutes and strain. Heat a

heavy-based pan, and sear the scallops on very high heat for about 20 seconds on each side.

To serve, remove the mousse from each mould by running a sharp knife around the edge and gently

turning out onto a plate. Place scallops on the side and spoon the strained sauce over the top of the

mousse. Garnish with the steamed spinach, coriander leaves and kaffir lime leaves.

[serves: 6]

recipe : tippy heng : toscanis

deep-fried cheese and tempura vegetables

For the tempura batter, put the egg into cold water and lightly beat,
adding the combined flours. Do not overwork batter.

Wrap cheese cubes with the cut nori sheet, sealing edges with a little
tempura batter. Dust wrapped cheese cubes and vegetables with flour.

Add vegetable oil to a pan, about 6 cm deep and heat to
approximately 160-180°C. Dip vegetables and wrapped cheese
into batter, then deep-fry until golden. Drain well.

Combine japanese soy, mirin and stock in a pan and bring
to the boil. Let cool to lukewarm.

Serve the tempura vegetables and deep-fried cheese with mixed
daikon and ginger, and dipping sauce on the side.

[serves: 4]

recipe : hideki takagi : misaki byron

ingredients:

200 gm cheddar cheese, cut into 2 cm cubes

2 nori sheets, cut into quarters

1 capsicum, 2 cm slices

4 celery leaves

12 beans

1/2 sweet potato, 1 cm slices

1 onion, sliced into 8 rings

1/2 eggplant, sliced into 8 rounds

1/4 cup self-raising flour

3 cups vegetable oil, for deep-frying

tempura batter:

1 whole egg

1 1/2 cups cold water

1 cup self-raising flour

1/5 cup potato starch or cornflour

dipping sauce:

100 ml japanese soy sauce

100 ml mirin

500 ml chicken or fish stock

condiments:

2 tablespoons grated daikon (japanese radish)

1 teaspoon grated ginger

"Byron Bay is cosmopolitan. It's the only place I can live in Australia, after Sydney, without feeling that life is passing me by."

Peter Powditch
artist

" **Byron is a feast** – for the eyes, the heart and the soul.

Every day here is a bonus.

I never take its beauty for granted,

which is why we fight to preserve it.

Byron's other secret ingredient is its people.

I'm sure we all feel the same – lucky and happy

to be here. I hope you can share days in Byron too. "

Di Morrissey
author

ingredients:

4 large potatoes, peeled and quartered

2 tablespoons cracked pepper

4 tablespoons butter, melted

1 cup illawarra plums

1 cup port

2 tablespoons sugar

4 venison fillets, trimmed

salt and pepper

2 tablespoons olive oil

2 bunches asparagus

300 gm rocket, washed

200 ml game stock

4 sprigs fresh thyme

venison tenderloin on potato and cracked pepper crumble with rocket, asparagus and illawarra plums

Boil potatoes until soft, drain and then mash. Combine mashed potato with cracked pepper and half the melted butter in a mixing bowl. Divide the mixture into four, and spoon into a 10 cm round mould, and place on a baking tray. Press down firmly on the top, and carefully slide off the mould to shape each crumble. Bake the potato crumbles in the oven at 250°C for 15 minutes.

Combine the plums, port and sugar in a small saucepan and bring to the boil. Reduce to medium heat, and reduce the mixture by half.

Season all sides of the venison fillet with salt and pepper. Heat half the olive oil in a heavy-based frypan, and then sear the venison on all sides. Remove and place on a baking tray. Bake in a preheated oven at 250°C for 5 minutes.

In a frypan, melt the remaining butter and olive oil over high heat. Sauté the asparagus for 1 minute. Reduce the heat to medium and add the rocket leaves until they become soft.

To serve, place the crumbles in the centre of four plates. Spread the rocket evenly around the crumbles. Slice the venison fillets and fan out on top of the crumbles. Tie the asparagus into bundles using sprigs of fresh thyme, and place them over the venison. Pour the heated game stock over the meat, then spoon the plum mixture over and around the entire dish.

[serves: 4]

recipe : marc romanella : boomerang

ingredients:

1/4 cup vegetable oil

4 chicken wings, tips removed
and cut in half at the joint

2 large onions, chopped

12 cloves garlic, chopped

3 dried shitaki mushrooms,
chopped and soaked in 1/4 cup
water (keep to add to stock)

1 cup jasmine rice

12 button mushrooms (if not
available, use regular field
mushrooms), chopped

20 gm hijiki seaweed

8 mussels in the shell, cleaned

12 japanese roe on scallops

12 green prawns, peeled and
de-veined (leave tails on)

2 small octopus or squid,
cleaned and cut into 4

1 1/2 cups chicken or fish stock

salt and pepper

1 tablespoon soy sauce

2 lemons, cut into wedges

seafood and chicken paella, japanese-style

Heat a teaspoon of vegetable oil in an ovenproof pot over medium heat. Add the chicken wings and fry until golden brown, remove from the pot. Add a little more oil then cook onion, garlic and shitaki mushrooms until soft. Add remaining oil and rice. Gently fry for a few minutes over medium heat, then replace cooked chicken wings in the pot. Add button mushrooms, hijiki seaweed, all of the seafood, stock and water from soaked shitaki mushrooms. Season with salt, pepper and soy sauce. Cover and bring to the boil over medium heat. Place pot in 190°C oven for approximately 20 minutes until all stock is absorbed. Remove from the oven, and rest for 10 minutes with the lid on. Serve with lemon wedges.

[serves: 4]

recipe : hideki takagi : misaki byron

ingredients:

1 kg rabbit

1 teaspoon cumin powder

100 ml vegetable oil

2 brown onions,
finely diced

2 cloves garlic, crushed

300 gm pumpkin,
1 cm dice

1 tablespoon sea salt

1 teaspoon cracked
black peppercorns

1 bunch silverbeet,
stalks removed

1 celery stalk, diced

1 large carrot, diced

300 ml red wine

1 bunch lemon thyme

6 bay leaves

10 whole peppercorns

500 ml water

1 tablespoon white sugar

10 sheets puff pastry

1 egg yolk

24 baby corn, steamed

onion jam:

3 brown onions, sliced

100 ml vegetable oil

1 cinnamon stick, roasted

10 cardamom pods, roasted and de-seeded

1 cup brown sugar

1 tablespoon sea salt

rabbit pie with spiced onion jam and steamed baby corn

Bone the rabbit and roughly dice the meat into 2 cm cubes. In a heavy-based pan, heat 50 ml of the oil and sauté half the onion and the garlic for 5 minutes. Next add the rabbit meat, pumpkin, cumin powder, salt and cracked pepper. Cook for a further 2 minutes, partially cooking the meat. Allow to cool. Blanch the silverbeet in boiling water for 30 seconds, and then refresh in cold water and drain.

Roast the rabbit bones in a hot oven until brown. In a large pot, heat the oil and sauté the remaining onion, celery and carrot until coloured, then add the red wine. When it has reduced by half, add the rabbit bones, 10 sprigs of lemon thyme, bay leaves, whole peppercorns and the water. Reduce this over medium heat, until it has a syrupy consistency. Strain the sauce, then season with salt, pepper, sugar and set aside.

Cut the pastry into rounds and line the base of 6 small non-stick pie tins. Place a thin layer of silverbeet in the bottom of each pie tin, and then fill with the rabbit mixture. Place another layer of silverbeet over the top, then cover the pies with a round of pastry to seal. Brush the edges and the top of the pastry with the egg yolk, and pierce a few holes in the top to allow the steam to escape whilst cooking. Bake in a preheated 200°C oven until golden brown.

To prepare the onion jam, sauté the sliced onion in a saucepan with the oil until slightly coloured. Pound the roasted cinnamon stick and cardamom pods in a mortar and pestle and add these, the brown sugar and salt to the onion mix. Stir for approximately 1 hour over low heat, until the onion mix has caramelised.

To serve, ladle the sauce onto the plates, place a pie in the centre of each. Place a spoonful of onion jam and the steamed baby corn beside the pies, and garnish with fresh sprigs of lemon thyme.

[serves: 6]

recipe : tippy heng : toscanis

crisp tasmanian salmon on a bed of puy lentils

Remove any bones from the salmon, and then cut each fillet
in half on the diagonal to form 8 even-sized triangles.

Place the lentils into a small saucepan, add enough water to cover by 8 cm.
Bring to the boil, then lower the heat and simmer for 12-15 minutes until
the lentils are nearly cooked, then drain. Combine the par-cooked lentils with
half a cup of wine in a saucepan and simmer for 5-8 minutes until the
wine has reduced and the lentils are tender, then season with salt.

Combine fish stock, remaining wine, orange and lime segments in a
saucepan. Bring to the boil, reduce heat and simmer for 25-30 minutes
until reduced to about 200 ml. Using a blender, process the citrus
reduction, adding the chopped butter until smooth.

Lightly grease a frypan and heat over high heat until very hot. Place
salmon, skin side down, and cook for 45 seconds. Turn over and
cook the other side for 45 seconds.

Place the lentil mixture in the centre of four plates. Top with two
pieces of salmon and spoon citrus reduction over the salmon.
Serve the salmon topped with a spoonful of salmon caviar.

[serves: 4]

recipe : marc romanella : boomerang

ingredients:

4 salmon fillets, skin on

250 gm puy lentils

500 ml dry white wine

125 ml fish stock

1 orange, segmented

1 lime, segmented

50 gm unsalted butter, chopped

75 gm salmon caviar

salt

Musicians and bands touring the east coast of Australia will play Sydney, Byron Bay and Brisbane, not because Byron is so profitable, but because they have friends here and it's a great place to enjoy a gig.

More than a decade of the huge **East Coast Blues Festival** with its international line-up has put Byron on the world map for blues fans. The **Byron Bay Writers Festival** is now an established national event, along with the others held in capital cities, and well-known authors queue to escape Sydney or Melbourne winters to mingle for a few days with their fans and peers in the August sunshine. Film-makers, scriptwriters, artists, photographers and journalists, experts in every creative field, can be found in the area, not usually making the same income they would in the city, but enjoying life far more.

This diverse population creates a vibrant community which attracts further visitors, and the shops, cafés and restaurants cater to us all. International stars or itinerant wanderers, everyone is free to enjoy the town.

It takes a lot to make a local look up from their latté.

ingredients:

1 1/2 kg butternut pumpkin,
peeled and cut into 2 cm dice

3 red capsicums

1/4 cup olive oil

1 large onion, chopped

2 celery sticks, chopped

2 cloves garlic, chopped

1 1/2 litres water

2 cups arborio rice

1/2 cup white wine

10 snowpeas

1 bunch continental parsley

1 bunch english spinach

30 gm pecorino cheese

20 gm butter

salt and pepper

50 gm sweet potato

1 cup vegetable oil

1/2 bunch rocket leaves

shaved pecorino cheese,
to garnish

pesto sauce:

20 gm pecorino cheese

1 bunch basil leaves

20 gm pinenuts

1/2 lemon, juiced

1 cup olive oil

2 cloves garlic

roasted sweet pumpkin, snowpea and baby spinach risotto

Drizzle olive oil over half the pumpkin and the capsicums, and roast them in a hot oven until the pumpkin is tender. When cooked, remove the skin and seeds from the capsicums and cut into strips. Reserve a third for the capsicum coulis.

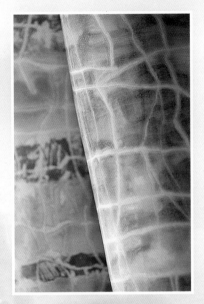

Sauté half the onion, celery and 1 clove of garlic until translucent. Add 1 litre of water and the remaining pumpkin. Cook until soft, then purée.

In a large pot, sauté the remaining onion and 1 clove of garlic until translucent. Add the arborio rice, stirring over heat until the rice starts to change colour. Add the white wine and reduce over low heat until all the wine is absorbed. Next add half a litre of water and bring to the boil. Simmer with the lid on, until all the water is absorbed. Remove from the heat and rest the covered rice for 10 minutes, before turning it out onto a tray to cool.

Place 1 cup of the puréed pumpkin (reserving half a cup for the capsicum coulis), and 2 cups of the cooked rice, into a large pot, and then gently stir in the roasted pumpkin, capsicum, snowpeas, parsley, english spinach, pecorino cheese, butter, salt and pepper.

To make the pesto sauce, mix all the pesto ingredients together in a blender until combined.

To make the capsicum coulis, blend the reserved capsicum and puréed pumpkin and season with salt and pepper.

Heat the remaining vegetable oil to about 165°C and deep-fry the sweet potato strips until crisp, then drain on kitchen paper.

Serve the risotto in the centre of a plate, with pesto sauce and red capsicum coulis around the edge, then top the risotto with rocket leaves, shaved pecorino cheese, and deep-fried sweet potato.

[serves: 4]

recipe : matthew gillespie : orient restaurant

ingredients:

3 pork hocks
(500-600 gm after boning)

3 cloves garlic

5 cm piece ginger, peeled
and thinly sliced

3 bay leaves

6 sprigs lemon thyme

1 cup dry white wine

1 litre water

1 litre vegetable oil

sauce:

2 kg veal bones

2 pig trotters

1 celery stick, roughly chopped

1 carrot, roughly chopped

3 bay leaves

6 sprigs thyme

12 whole black peppercorns

1 tablespoon tomato paste

1 litre red wine

1 litre water

150 gm enoki mushrooms

150 gm oyster mushrooms

200 gm swiss brown mushrooms

100 gm dried black fungus,
soaked and washed

salt and pepper

galette:

6 medium potatoes,
peeled and thinly sliced

100 gm butter, melted

200 ml cream

salt and pepper

mousse:

1 bunch english spinach,
washed and trimmed

1 gelatine sheet

250 ml cream

salt and pepper

braised pork hock with potato galette, spinach mousse and assorted mushroom sauce

Roll the boned hocks into a sausage shape with the skin on the outside. Wrap the hocks in muslin and tie with string to secure. Place them into a saucepan with the garlic, ginger, bay leaves, thyme, white wine and water. Cover the pan and cook over low heat for 3 hours, turning the hocks occasionally. When cooked remove the hocks and refrigerate until they have set firm. Remove muslin and string, dry and then cut each hock into four thick slices. Heat the oil in a large pot and deep-fry hocks for 7-10 minutes. Drain on paper towels and keep warm until needed.

In a large baking tray, place the veal bones, pig trotters, celery, carrot, bay leaves, thyme, peppercorns and tomato paste. Roast in a hot oven for 30 minutes until brown, then remove the pan from the oven. Place on the stove, and then add the red wine. Reduce over low heat until reduced to one-third, then add the water and reduce by a further one-third. Strain into a saucepan, and then add the chopped mushrooms, salt and pepper. Simmer for approximately 1 minute.

Arrange layers of thinly sliced potato, slightly overlapping, with the melted butter around a small pan. Drizzle the cream over the top, season with salt and pepper, and bake in a 180°C oven for 30 minutes until golden brown.

To prepare the mousse, blanch the spinach in boiling water for 5 seconds and refresh immediately in iced water. Blend the spinach in a food processor, and slowly add the cream whilst the motor is running. Soak the gelatine leaf in cold water, drain and then dissolve the gelatine in the microwave oven for 20 seconds. Fold the gelatine through the spinach cream, season with salt and pepper, and allow to set in the refrigerator.

To serve, place two slices of pork hock on a serve of the potato galette, spoon the spinach mousse on the top, and pour the mushroom sauce around the plate.

[serves: 6]

recipe : tippy heng : toscanis

ingredients:

250 gm wild rice, boiled until almost tender

1 egg, beaten

1/3 cup plain flour

2 tablespoons olive oil

4 large duckling breasts, deboned and skin removed

salt and pepper

200 ml chicken stock

25 gm salted black beans

1 tablespoon butter

1 lemon grass stalk, very finely diced

1 tablespoon dried wakame

400 gm mushrooms
(shitake, wood ear, oyster, portobello)

1/2 cup olive oil

1 leek, cut into long fine strips

roasted breast of duckling on wild rice cakes with mushrooms and black bean sauce

Combine cooked wild rice, egg and flour in a mixing bowl, divide into four patties. In a non-stick pan, heat a tablespoon of olive oil on high and fry each rice cake individually for 1 minute on each side, being careful not to break them, and set aside. Season both sides of duckling breasts with salt and pepper. In the same pan, heat 1 tablespoon olive oil on high and sear each breast for 45 seconds per side. Place both duckling and rice cakes on a flat baking tray and roast in preheated oven at 250°C for 6-7 minutes.

In a saucepan, combine chicken stock and washed black beans.
Simmer on low heat for approximately 10 minutes.

Melt 1 tablespoon of butter in the pan on high heat. Sauté lemon grass and wakame for 30 seconds, then add sliced mushrooms and cook until tender.

In a pan, heat half a cup of olive oil and fry leeks until crisp.
Remove from oil, drain and season with salt and pepper.

Place rice cakes on individual plates, spoon mushrooms over each.
Slice duckling breasts into 5 pieces and fan out over the top of mushrooms.
Spoon black bean sauce over duckling and garnish with fried leek.

[serves: 4]

recipe : marc romanella : boomerang

layered white and dark chocolate mousse with raspberry and cointreau jelly and chocolate ice-cream cones

To make the ice-cream: In a saucepan, heat the milk, 250 ml of cream and the honey, until starting to simmer. Remove from the heat and stir in the chocolate. Whisk the egg yolks and the sugar in a bowl until light and creamy, and then pour in the chocolate mix, whisking continuously. Place the bowl over a pot of simmering water, and stir the mixture for about 25 minutes, until it coats the back of a spoon. Strain the custard and allow to cool completely. Stir in the remaining cream and churn in an ice-cream machine until firm enough to hold its shape. Line the inside of six 12 cm x 4 cm metal pastry horns with baking paper. Fill a piping bag with the ice-cream, and then pipe into the lined moulds, almost to the top. Tap gently to ensure that there are no trapped air bubbles, then freeze for 5 hours.

To make the jelly: In a saucepan, gently simmer the orange juice and sugar. Soak the gelatine leaves in cold water and then squeeze out the excess water. Stir the cointreau and the softened gelatine into the hot juice until dissolved. Pass the liquid through a fine sieve, then pour into 150 ml dome-shaped moulds. Allow to set slightly, then place a raspberry in the centre of each, and refrigerate until set.

To make the mousse: In a saucepan, bring the milk to a simmer. Whisk the egg yolks and sugar in a bowl until light and creamy, and then pour the warm milk into the egg mixture whisking continuously. Soften the gelatine leaves in cold water, squeeze out the excess water and stir into the egg mixture until dissolved. Place the bowl over a saucepan of simmering water, whisking until the mixture coats the back of a spoon. Strain through a fine sieve. Divide the mixture into two equal amounts. Place the white and dark chocolate into two separate bowls, and place these over a saucepan of simmering water to melt chocolate. Stir the divided egg mixture into each of the bowls of melted chocolate and stir until thickened. Refrigerate until cool, then fold the whipped cream into each chocolate mix.

Remove the set jelly moulds from the refrigerator, and fill the moulds, one layer at a time, with the white and dark mousse. Allow the first layer to set before proceeding with the next, then let the moulds completely set before serving.

To serve, heat the set moulds slightly over hot water, and turn onto plates. Remove the ice-cream cones from the horn moulds and stand ice-cream next to the mousse. If desired, pipe a swirl of chocolate sauce around plate.

[serves: 6]

136

ingredients:

ice-cream:

250 ml milk

500 ml cream

50 gm honey

250 gm dark couverture chocolate

6 large eggs

200 gm castor sugar

jelly:

250 ml orange juice

85 gm castor sugar

3 gelatine leaves

50 ml cointreau

6 raspberries

mousse:

200 ml milk

4 egg yolks

100 gm castor sugar

3 gelatine leaves

200 gm dark couverture chocolate

200 gm white couverture chocolate

300 ml whipped cream

chocolate sauce (optional)

recipe : tippy heng : toscanis

"Occasionally I like to picture bohemian Lord Byron uproariously enjoying the rich rainforests, flamboyant sunsets and azure waters of his future 'namesake' – Australia's favourite playground of dolphins and other pleasure-seekers. Blessed with a natural abundance of eating, drinking and feasting ingredients, the Bay has always been a celebration place for its traditional Aboriginal inhabitants.

Evocative Byron flavours – coconut oil on salty skin, bush spices, Peruvian parsnips, Japanese artichokes and purple potatoes from sun-soaked permaculture gardens – all pay fitting tribute to Lord B's credo that *the best of life is but intoxication...*"

Lilith
astrologer

There are many tribes that make up Byron Bay. A few live in stunning houses overlooking glorious beaches or in country retreats featured in glossy magazines; a few more live in teepees, or caravans or handbuilt houses on multiple occupancies, but most live in ordinary houses. Perhaps they could be described as seeking ordinary lives, the type of life which now seems unavailable in the city. **The freedom to live a quiet, balanced and healthy lifestyle in such a beautiful location is anything but ordinary in this world.** In Byron Bay it is possible.

photo captions

recipe index

featured restaurants:

featured guesthouses:

other recipes from:

Along with the above, Byron Shire has many other great places to eat.